IMAGES
of America
PAYSON

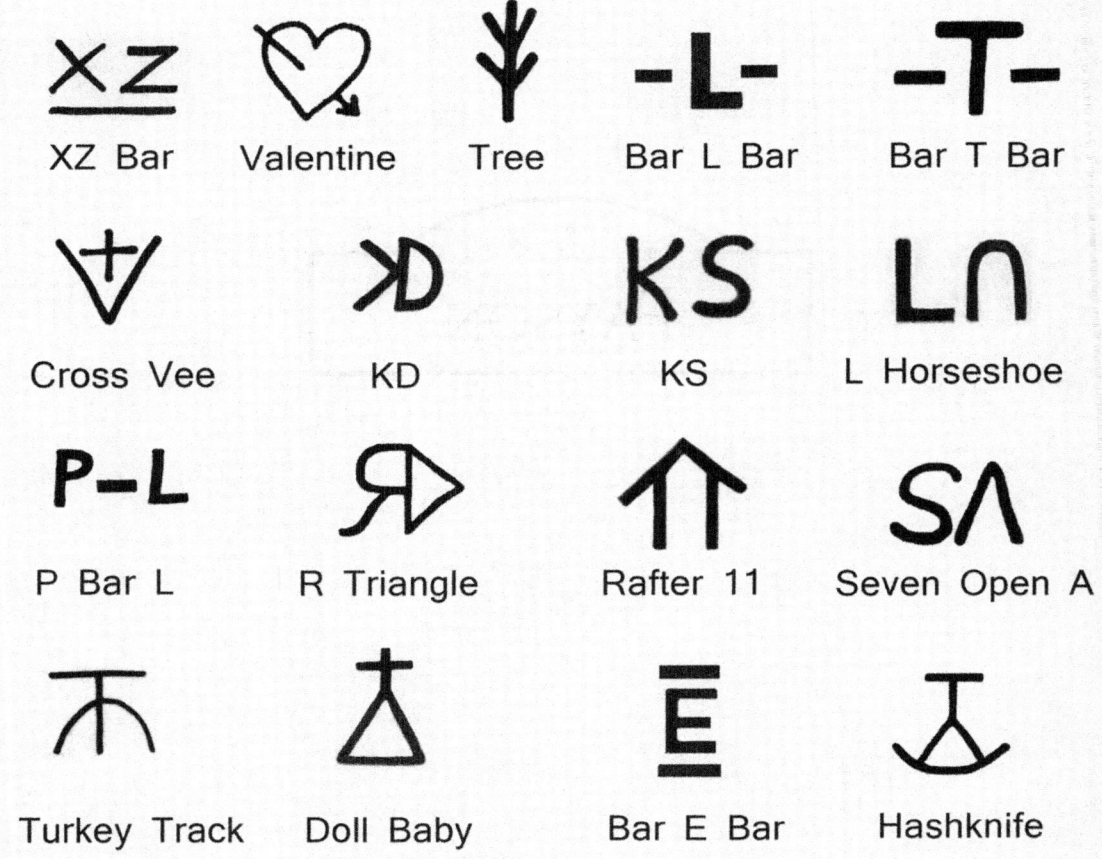

Cattle-branding logos in Payson, Arizona, were very important to cattle ranchers in order to maintain their livestock.

ON THE COVER: This c. 1900 photograph is well known by the old-timers in Payson. It is called "A Full House - Three Jokers and a Pair of Jacks." Payson was known far and wide for its gambling and betting on horse races. On the left is the old Pieper Saloon, now called Bootleg Alley Antiques. During the days of Prohibition, the well inside this old saloon was used to hide bootleg whiskey from the prohis. To the right is the old Tammany Hall, owned and operated by Judge John Wentworth. Wentworth married Katherine Houston here in 1890, and Ida "Sis" Haught married Henry Garrels here in 1913, so we know the approximate years of Wentworth's Tammany Hall, named after New York's famous Tammany Hall. Bill Boardman is pictured on the left at age 16, and Washington "Wash" Gibson is on the right at age 30. According to the writing on the back of the photograph, the man in the middle is supposedly Hook Larson, but we have a confirmed photograph of Hook Larsen and this is not the same man. So the joker in the middle is a wild card!

Images of America
PAYSON

Jayne Peace Pyle and Jinx Pyle

Copyright © 2010 by Jayne Peace Pyle and Jinx Pyle
ISBN 978-1-5316-5637-9

Published by Arcadia Publishing
Charleston, South Carolina

Library of Congress Control Number: 2009938752

For all general information contact Arcadia Publishing at:
Telephone 843-853-2070
Fax 843-853-0044
E-mail sales@arcadiapublishing.com
For customer service and orders:
Toll-Free 1-888-313-2665

Visit us on the Internet at www.arcadiapublishing.com

*In honor of the tough-souled, hearty pioneering families
and their descendants who settled in northern
Gila County from the 1870s to the present*

Contents

Acknowledgments		6
Introduction		7
1.	The Ancients and the Apaches	9
2.	Ranches and Cowboys	19
3.	Zane Grey and Hunters Under the Tonto Rim	31
4.	Rodeo	45
5.	Mining and Logging	57
6.	Payson Area Personalities	69
7.	Natural Bridge	79
8.	Transportation	91
9.	Water	103
10.	Payson Buildings	115

Acknowledgments

Our sincere thanks goes to Sandy Carson of the Northern Gila County Historical Society who loaned us photographs for this book. Not only did she loan them, she scanned them and did her best to find just the photographs we needed. All photographs marked NGCHS belong to the Northern Gila County Historical Society. Our thanks also to Pat Randall of Payson who let us dig through her photographs and use what we wanted. Her photographs are marked Pat Randall. Ella Lee Owens and Jim Skinner also deserve thanks for loaning us photographs of early Payson that have never before been in print. Ella Lee and Jim's photographs have been given photograph credits as well. We are very thankful that we inherited the Anna Mae Deming photograph collection. Anna Mae's photographs, plus both of our family collections (Peace and Pyle), provide us with a lot of history. Our thanks go to Marshall Trimble for suggesting us as the authors of this book. And our thanks to Jared Jackson of Arcadia Publishing for prodding us along on this project. He has been great! We are sincerely grateful to all who helped with this book in any way. Payson deserves to have its own Arcadia book!

Introduction

Payson, Arizona, is blessed with a history as unique and untamed as the pioneers who settled it. The first attention given to what, in 1884, would begin to be known as Payson, was by the U.S. Army. A need for a fort between Camp Verde and Fort Thomas was thought to be of paramount importance if the Tonto Apaches were to be subjugated so that the Tonto Basin could be opened for settlement. The army's idea to build a fort in the very heart of Apache country was soon dismissed, however, when it became apparent that it would be impossible to keep supply lines open in the heart of the Tonto Basin, then known as Apacheria.

In 1874, with the Apaches at least partly subdued, the settlement of the Tonto Basin could begin. Bordered on the north by the Mogollon Rim, on the south by what is now Roosevelt Lake, on the west by the Mazatzal Range, and on the east by the Sierra Anchas, the basin is about 50 miles long and an average of 20 miles wide.

Pioneer cattlemen came into the area, along with an equal number of prospectors. The ranchers staked out their claims (160 acres), built a log cabin, and brought in cattle. Ranges were unfenced so the cattle mingled, and it was necessary to have a community roundup of the stock in order to brand the calves, take a tally, and drive the sale cattle to market.

The prospectors roamed the entire basin, but most were drawn to the mineral-rich country from Wild Rye Creek north to the top of Oxbow Hill. In 1881, a miner's settlement known as Marysville was established about 3 miles southwest of present-day Payson.

Payson first appeared on Arizona Territorial maps as the "Burch Ranch" because, in 1876, William Burch, the first settler, had established a ranch in the valley of grass and tall ponderosa pine trees. Two years later, William McDonald joined Burch; then as others saw the beauty of the land, the abundance of water, and the grass for cattle, here they came! The valley where Burch's Ranch was located became a roundup camp every fall and spring, as it was a natural gathering place and holding ground for cattle. Anywhere cowboys gather is likely to be a place of practical jokes, contests, and gambling, and so it was at the roundup camps near the Burch Ranch.

By 1882, a few folks had moved to the area surrounding Burch's Ranch. John C. Callahan had a blacksmith shop, and John Hise had a general store. The two men laid out a town site, and the place was aptly called Green Valley. By 1884, Hise and Callahan, with aid from an Illinois representative by the name of Edwin Payson, had applied for and been granted a post office. It proved awkward addressing mail to the Payson Post Office in Green Valley, so the town adopted the name of Payson.

The little community wished to celebrate their accomplishments, and the cowboys passed along word to the ranchers that there would be some "doins" the third week of August in 1884. Arizona Charley Meadows had a hand in the celebration activities and initiated some cowboy bronc-riding and roping events along with horse racing. This was the first of a continuous string of rodeos that to date (2009) has lasted for 125 years.

The mining industry in the Tonto Basin provided a livable income for many, and a few men made their fortunes. Logging and timber also played a vital roll in Payson's economy from its conception. During the 1950s, Owens Brothers Lumber moved their operation from the outlying area into Payson. They expanded their operation and had about 60 workers on their payroll, but neither mining nor timber rivaled the cattle industry in the Tonto Basin.

For most of Payson's existence, a trip to Phoenix was a major undertaking. Even after the Bush Highway was finally completed from Payson to Phoenix in the 1940s, it was still an eight-hour drive, and Payson remained relatively isolated from the rest of the world. Then in 1958, the Beeline Highway was completed and paved between Payson and Phoenix. The Rim Country was then accessible to those in the Salt River Valley and Phoenix. Payson's cooler temperatures, pine trees, fishing, and hunting drew folks from the desert like nails to a magnet.

Starting in about 1958, Payson began a transition from a cow town to a tourist and retirement community that is still evolving as this book is being written. The cattle, logging, and mining industries have been all but eradicated from Payson and the entire Tonto Basin.

Say "Payson" today and the name will bring many different thoughts to the minds of those who know it. Old-timers still like to recall it as a cow town. They remember the Payson rodeos when the best rodeo cowboys in the world came to town. They remember a wide-open town of friendly people who would share their homes, food, and coffee with all who came to the August Doin's. They remember the great horse races and the horses—Buster, Prissy, Brown Bomber, Crusader, and more.

Many outdoorsmen remember Payson as the hub of a great trout fishing and hunting area, where deer, elk, mountain lions, and bears roamed the forests. Others think of Payson as a great retirement community where the average year-round temperature is 70 degrees. For whatever reason, all who know the town seem to hold it in fond regard. Gene Pyle, an old Payson cowboy, may have put it best when he said, "There are two kinds of people in Arizona, those who live in Payson and those who wish they did."

One

THE ANCIENTS AND THE APACHES

The prehistoric culture known as the Mogollon lived in the southwest from approximately 150 AD until about 1450 AD. The name archaeologists have given this culture is derived from the Mogollon Mountains, which were named after Don Juan Ignacio Flores Mogollón, the Spanish governor of New Mexico in the early 1700s.

The Mogollon people were mostly agriculturalists, but some depended on hunting and gathering for survival. They built small pit homes near their fields. As their culture advanced and the need for defense increased, they began to build larger multistoried buildings.

It is believed that sometime between 900 and 1100 AD, the Anasazi culture absorbed much of the Mogollon culture, merging traits. It is also believed that this merged culture contributed to the cultural background of the Hopi, Zuni, and Acoma.

By 1500, a large number of people called Apache had pushed into the Tonto Basin. They were not farmers but savage warriors and hunters. Their warlike tactics stemmed from the necessity of survival. They had once roamed the plains, but as European Americans pushed west, French and British traders supplied guns and ammunition to tribes who were enemies of the Apaches. The Apaches suffered great defeats and fled to the southwest to survive.

The northward advance of the Spaniards ran head on into Apache country. Spanish expeditions invaded Apache territory as early as 1540, when Coronado searched for the Seven Cities of Gold. For years the Apaches struggled to survive between the Spaniards and other American Indian tribes, both of who were armed and mounted.

Slowly the Apaches acquired firearms from the Spanish along with ammunition, clothing, hats, and metal tools. They took what they needed during raids, including livestock.

At the beginning of the Apache Wars most of the Arizona-New Mexico Territory was called Apacheria, meaning Apache Land. As the U.S. Army overpowered the various Apache bands and placed them on reservations, Gila County was called Apacheria. Finally, only the Tonto Basin, bordered on the north by the Mogollon Rim, on the west by the Mazatzals, on the south by Salt River Canyon, and on the east by the Sierra Anchas, was referred to as Apacheria—the final Apache stronghold in the United States.

Metates on the rim of Conley Point overlooking the East Verde River were used first by the Mogollon Culture, then later by the Apaches. Often used to grind corn into meal, they were also used by the Apaches to grind the roasted acorns of the blackjack oak, white oak, and bush acorns into a flour from which thick, nutritious soup could be made. The root of the needle-pointed Mescal (shown above) was a major source of food for the Mogollon Culture and the Apaches. The roots, available year-round, were dug and then roasted in Mescal pits covered with hot rocks. (Photograph by Sandy Carson, courtesy NGCHS.)

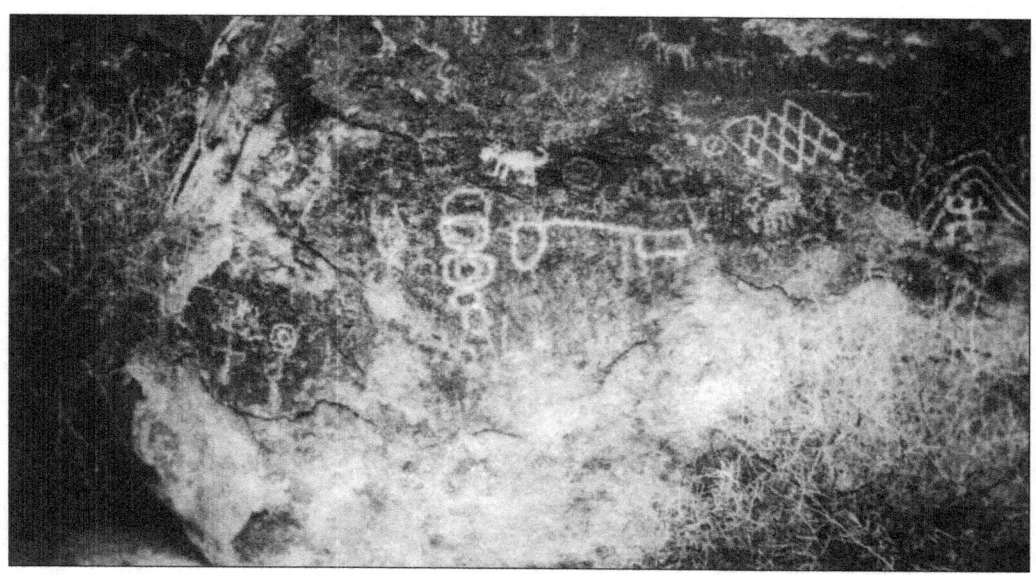

The Mogollon Culture was well established in what is now Arizona thousands of years before Europeans arrived in the region. Here we find more evidence of their early life depicting both men and animals. These petroglyphs are typical of those found in the Mogollon Rim Country. (Both courtesy NGCHS.)

Establishing sedentary societies in Arizona in the first century AD, the Anasazi and Mogollon cultures were ancestors of the Pueblo Indians. They grew beans, corn, and squash. About 400 AD, these cultures began making pottery for cooking and storing water, and they planted yucca and cotton that was woven into clothing. Shown here are the Tonto Cliff Dwellings from different angles as they were photographed in 1920.

These petroglyphs, resembling human feet, can be found a few miles south of Payson. Ox Bow Hill, between Payson and Rye Creek, is rich in artifacts of the Mogollon culture. The early white settlers found stone ax heads and arrowheads, and many collected the metates and manos of those who came before. (NGCHS.)

History tells us that Fr. Eusebio Kino, a Jesuit priest, came to Arizona in 1692. The first Spanish settlement was constructed in Arizona at Tubac in 1752, and the first Spanish fort was built at Tucson in 1776. The Spanish explorers were ever in pursuit of gold, and the ancient fort above is evidence of their exploration of central Arizona. The fort is typical of several in the Mazatzal Mountain Range, which runs from North Peak, near Payson, to Four Peaks, a towering monument over the Valley of the Sun. (Photograph by Sandy Carson, courtesy NGCHS.)

The Basin of the Tonto Apaches, bordered on the north by the Mogollon Rim, on the west by the Mazatzals, on the south by Salt River Canyon, and on the east by the Sierra Anchas, was the final stronghold of the Apaches within the U.S. territories. These wikiups, pictured near Roosevelt in 1909, were made of hides stretched over bent willow branches and differed little from those in the Northern Tonto Basin near Payson. (Photograph by Anna Mae Deming, courtesy NGCHS.)

The Tonto Apaches used whatever material was on hand to build their wikiups; the above center wikiup appears to be built Tonto fashion and then covered with tarps tied on with ropes. Usually a fire pit was dug and lined with rocks, and the wikiup was built around the fire pit. The Apache version was constructed by leaning poles or saplings together in a tepee fashion and weaving bear grass between the poles, after which more grass was woven in vertically to allow the structure to shed water. These were built north of Payson in the Houston Mesa area in the early 1900s. (Photograph by Olinger, courtesy NGCHS.)

Dressed in hunting regalia, this Apache man poses for the camera with his bow and arrow on the San Carlos Reservation, near Globe, Arizona, around 1900. (Peace-Pyle collection.)

Nana, a leader of the Warm Springs Apaches and a brother-in-law of Geronimo, went on a retaliatory raid in 1881 in Mexico, New Mexico Territory, and Arizona. In two months, the old but relentless Nana and his followers rode about 3,000 miles and fought a number of battles and skirmishes with minimal casualties. Much of the stock taken during the raids was traded to Juh's band when the two Apache groups met in the Sierra Madre Mountains of Mexico a few months later. Nana surrendered to George Crook in 1883 but bolted the reservation with Geronimo two years later. In 1886, Nana finally surrendered to Crook again. After spending the last 10 years of his life as a prisoner, Nana would die at Fort Sill, Oklahoma Territory, in 1896. They guessed his age to be about 80. (Peace-Pyle collection.)

The Apache Kid was born about 1860 on the San Carlos Reservation. He worked as a scout under Al Sieber and, by 1882, had become a sergeant. In 1887, the Apache Kid went in search of a man he believed had killed his father. Things went downhill for the "Kid" after this. He was found guilty of murder and was sentenced to seven years in Yuma Territorial Prison. While being transported to the prison, the Kid escaped. During the fighting that took place, three guards—Glenn Reynolds, Eugene Middleton, and W. A. Holmes—were killed. Over the next few years, the Apache Kid was accused of many crimes, but it would have been impossible for him to commit all of them. A reward of $5,000 for his capture, dead or alive, was promised by the Arizona territorial legislature, but he was not found. Some think he went to Mexico and lived to an old age. (Peace-Pyle collection.)

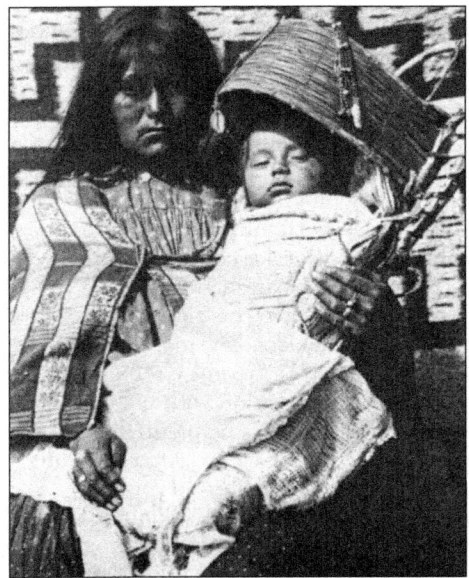

Apache women put their babies in cradle-boards right after they were born, and this is where they stayed most of the time until they could walk. Most cradle-boards were made of willow branches, but other types of wood were used. A single curved hoop at the top made it easy for the mother to carry the child or hang the cradle-board in a tree. Flat slats of lightweight wood were laid across the hoop, making a backboard. The head cover was made of woven cottonwood branches that created an arch for protection from the sun and rain. The cradle-board was then covered in soft deer hide or, in later years, cloth. (Peace-Pyle collection.)

This child appears to be carried by his mother, a Tonto Apache woman, in a cloth sling on her back, which indicates this photograph was probably taken in the 1920s. (Peace-Pyle collection.)

Geronimo is on the far right of this photograph along with three other Apache warriors. These photographs were taken on the San Carlos Indian Reservation. Note the men were dressed in cloth, although they tried to retain the Apache style. (Peace-Pyle collection.)

Geronimo, called Goyathlay at birth, was born in western New Mexico in 1829. He married a Chiricahua Apache and had three children. Once when he was away, Mexican soldiers killed his aged mother, his wife, and his three young children. These acts changed his life. He vowed to kill every Mexican and American who entered Apache land. Mexican soldiers called him Geronimo, in honor of Saint Jerome, after watching his daring feats in battle. They thought he was somehow protected from bullets. Since he was not a Chiricahua, he could not be a chief but often spoke for his brother-in-law, Juh, a Chiricahua chief. His sister, Nah-dos-te, married prominent Warm Springs Apache leader Nana. The last American Indian fighting force to formally surrender to the U.S. Army was led by Geronimo. Because he fought against all odds and was the last to surrender, he became the most famous Apache leader. He was taken into custody in 1886 and died at the Fort Sill Army Post in Oklahoma in February 1909, after 22 years as a prisoner of war. (Peace-Pyle collection.)

Two

RANCHES AND COWBOYS

Many soldiers, having seen the beauty, minerals, and rich ranch land, returned home to tell their families of the wonderful basin of the Tontos. Word spread and regardless of any danger the Apaches still presented, the lure of Tonto Basin with its rich grass-filled valleys, promising mineral outcroppings, and dark canyons shielding rushing mountain streams proved irresistible to white settlers.

The miners and cattlemen were soon arriving in the Tonto Basin, which included what is now Payson. Until the mid-1880s, mining was as strong as cattle ranching, but thereafter ranching began to dominate Rim Country and Tonto Basin industry for over half a century.

This remained the situation through the 1950s as the ranching industry supported the businesses in Payson. Local ranchers sold their sale cattle and spent their money in Payson. They paid the teacher, the preacher, the grocery man, and the blacksmith and bought food, clothing, and services.

For the most part, Payson-area ranchers were straight-shooting individuals with neighbors or strangers. Their handshakes were as good as their signatures. They asked no quarter but shared with neighbors or strangers. Ranching was their occupation, their religion, and a large part of their social life.

A. T. Vaughn and his son, Jack (right), are pictured in front of this old Star Valley ranch house that was built in the late 1800s. It was owned by the Azbills, Houston brothers, Fullers, a partnership of Floyd Pyle and John and Nellie Beard, A. T. Vaughn, Clifford Martin, Austin Haught, Raymond Cline, and others. It ran under the following brands: U Bar, P Bar L, Cross V, and 7A. (Courtesy Mary Vaughn Rogers.)

Thousands of head of cattle were shipped from these corrals owned by C. A. "Bud" Jones. Bud burned the S Open A brand on his cattle, and his ranch headquarters were just west of Payson. The S. A. Ranch had the first set of cattle scales in the Payson area, and many other ranchers took advantage of this convenience, driving their sale cattle to the S. A.'s to weigh and ship them. (Peace-Pyle collection.)

Shown here is C. A. "Bud" Jones, longtime owner of the S Open A Ranch near Payson. (Courtesy Stuart Jones.)

This four-bedroom log cabin, at the Myrtle Ranch on Ellison Creek under the Mogollon Rim, was built to accommodate the many hunting parties that visited the ranch. Although the Myrtle Ranch was a working cattle ranch, the Pyles were well-known lion- and bear-hunting guides. (Peace-Pyle collection.)

The main house at the Myrtle Ranch was originally built to be the main hunting lodge. The Pyles soon learned that people would pay for hunting guides, so the cattle money was supplemented with a guide service. (Peace-Pyle collection.)

George Cline excelled at anything he tried. He was a highly successful rancher, a noted racehorse man, a world-champion roper, and one of the best all-around cowboys in Payson and the Tonto Basin. He owned and ran half a dozen ranches in his lifetime, including the T Turkey Track and the Bouquet. He raised and sold thousands of head of cattle, and if he really liked someone, he would refer to that person as the "gen-u-ine article." George Cline was the "Genuine Article!" (Peace-Pyle collection.)

Roxie Cline was the wife and companion of Gila County rancher George Cline. She could make a house a home, bake wonderful Dutch oven biscuits, cut T-bone steaks from a beef loin, punch cows with the boys, or cuss out a hound dog. She also sang her favorite song, that "Gol-Darn Wheel." George referred to her as "Blossom" all of their married years. (Peace-Pyle collection.)

The old ranch house at the Doll Baby still stands today (2009) near where Pine Creek makes its junction with the East Verde River. The ranch name was derived from the Cross Triangle Brand. The cross over the triangle was said by a little girl to look like her doll baby. (Peace-Pyle collection.)

Dick Taylor is pictured here in his town hat, but don't let that fool you at all. He was a cowboy, rough and tough as they come. Taylor once treed a mountain lion and, without a gun, tied his pocketknife to a mescal pole, climbed the tree, and cut the lion's throat, eventually killing him. (Peace-Pyle collection.)

This old barn is reminiscent of the days when Payson was a cattle town. The ranch where it stands, now within the present town limits of Payson, was owned by Turkey Thompson, the Chilsons, the Willy Wade family, and Fritz Taylor during the 1970s, when the picture was taken. (Peace-Pyle collection.)

Payson cowboys had their fun. They spent many hours on horseback and often trained their horses to do tricks on cue. Here Robert Hale is showing off a little in front of friends. (Peace-Pyle collection.)

During the early days of cattle ranching in and around Payson, corrals and fences were luxuries not always available. Often cattle were just held in a herd by cowboys while a branding crew dragged the calves to the fire to brand, earmark, dehorn, and perform any other needed operations on the calves. Robert Hale is shown here south of Payson near Rye dehorning a Bar T Bar Calf. (Peace-Pyle collection.)

This old ranch, founded by early Mormon settlers in 1878, was first owned by the Sanders family. In 1891, they traded it to William "Will" Neal. Perlie Ellison, son of Col. Jesse Ellison who lived at the Q Ranch near Pleasant Valley, once owned part of the ranch for a short time. The Ellisons liked the lower country of Gisela for the longer growing season. When Ellison left, Neal bought that part of the ranch back. Will Neal's son, Riley Neal, ran the ranch until 1960, when it was sold to Will's granddaughter, Anna Mae Hale Peace, and her husband, Calvin Peace. Nine months of growing season, abundant water from Tonto Creek, and rich bottomland soil made it a very desirable ranch headquarters. (Peace-Pyle collection.)

Rancher, cowboy, and former Texas Ranger, Will Neal came from Texas into New Mexico driving 500 head of cattle in 1885. He lost his cattle when he had to flee New Mexico after a gunfight but made it safely into Globe with his family. After a short stint in the freighting business, he acquired a ranch in April 1891 in the Gisela Valley south of Payson. He drowned while trying to cross Tonto Creek during a flood in the spring of 1905. (Peace-Pyle collection.)

Calvin Peace was raised in Pleasant Valley, where he worked on various ranches including the old Graham Ranch of Pleasant Valley War fame. The ranch was owned by the Young sisters, for whom the town and post office are named. Calvin married Anna Mae Hale and ranched in Gisela on the old Sam Haught place, then on the Neal Ranch after serving in World War II. (Photograph by Alice Wrobley, courtesy Peace-Pyle collection.)

Perlie Ellison, shown here with a bear across his saddle horse, was a rancher, miner, and cowboy. He did whatever it took to "skin the cat." He was the son of Col. Jesse Ellison and father of noted cowboy author, Slim Ellison. Horseback is Perlie's brother, Jesse Ellison. Perlie and his wife, Lula, moved from his father's Q Ranch near Canyon Creek to Gisela in 1898 with their two sons, Glenn "Slim" and Nathan. They bought 30 acres of the Neal ranch where the early Mormons had planted 300 fruit trees. There was no fruit on the Q Ranch at the time, so Colonel Ellison brought his wife and other womenfolk over to Gisela to pick fruit. They dried it and canned it, then packed it on horses and took it back to the Q Ranch. (Courtesy Peace-Pyle collection.)

This photograph shows part of the old Belluzzi Place, later called the Rim Trail Ranch. It is located under the Mogollon Rim on the East Verde River. It was never headquarters for more than a few head of cattle, but apple and other fruit trees grew in abundance and it is a beautiful place. (Courtesy NGCHS.)

Hy Fuller and John Lazear hold a heard of cattle on top of the Mogollon Rim during the 1915 roundup at the Moqui Ranch. Many Payson-area ranchers ran cattle on top of the Mogollon during the summer months, but during the winter, snow covered the mountain in depths that often exceeded 6 feet. (Peace-Pyle collection.)

Cattle that ranged on top of the Mogollon Rim during the summer months were often separated from the sale cattle being driven to the railroads in Flagstaff or Winslow. The mother herd would then be driven back to winter range under the Mogollon. The photograph above shows Lazear cattle being worked (separated) at the Willow Valley Corrals on top of the Rim. (Peace-Pyle collection.)

Every Rim Country, Payson, or Tonto Basin cowboy worthy of the name could shoe a horse. A very few of the outlying ranches had a full-time blacksmith. Most of the early-day ranchers and cowboys could do a little blacksmithing and were expected to shoe their own string of horses. Here Normand Winters tacks one on a cow pony. (Peace-Pyle collection.)

Three

Zane Grey and Hunters Under the Tonto Rim

Zane Grey first came to the Mogollon Rim Country with his hunting guide, Al Doyle, in 1918. He came for two main reasons: He wanted to hunt bear, mountain lion, and turkey, and he wanted to hear the stories of the Pleasant Valley War of the 1880s.

Grey and Doyle rode from Flagstaff, dropped off the Rim at Nash Point, then rode into Payson and camped near the middle of town. Grey was looking for Fred Haught, who had worked at the Ashurst Ranch with Al Doyle, but the first Haught he met was Anderson Lee "Babe" Haught, a cousin of Fred's. Grey and Doyle followed Babe Haught to his ranch under the Mogollon Rim, and Grey was taken with the beauty of the place. Here he would write and hunt almost every fall for the next 10 years. He hired the Haughts to build him a cabin, and from the scenic view of his porch, he drew upon the magnificent surroundings that inspired many of his western novels.

Bears, lions, and other animals abounded in the still-wild country under the Mogollon Rim. Grey was hooked. He hired Babe Haught and his three sons—Edd, George, and Richard—as hunting guides. Grey won the friendship of the Babe Haught family and that of several of his neighbors, including Elwood Pyle and sons, Lewie, and Floyd.

On his third trip to the Tonto, Babe Haught took the author to Pleasant Valley where he visited with Fred Haught and Sam Haught. They spoke of the war in general terms, but Grey learned little, as the old-timers did not talk details about the war. Grey's book would be fiction.

He returned to the Mogollon Rim Country during the autumn months to observe the characters, culture, and stories of the people. He hunted, fished, and loved the solitude and atmosphere that inspired him to write. His cabin burned in the Dude Fire of 1990, but a replica of it was built beside the Northern Gila County Historical Society Museum in Payson in 2005.

The famous author Zane Grey spent considerable time at his cabin under the Tonto Rim. Of his 66 western novels, 13 of those were set in the Rim Country with 27 total set in Arizona. He wrote *Code of the West* based on the Henry "Pappy" Haught family, *Under the Tonto Rim* was based on the Anderson L. "Babe" Haught family, and *Arizona Ames* was based on life in the Tonto Basin. He got the idea for his book *Twin Sombreros* after he met the Pyle twins, Myrth and Myrl. Many of the characters he met in the Rim Country became featured characters in several of his western novels. *Tales of Lonely Trails* is not fiction. Volume two of this book is stories about people under the Mogollon Rim. (Peace-Pyle collection.)

Anderson Lee "Babe" Haught, the official guide of Zane Grey in Arizona during the 1920s, took many black bear from under the Mogollon Rim. Black bear were numerous in the early days and often became stock killers. (Peace-Pyle collection.)

These two bear cubs were captured by Floyd Pyle and were given to Zane Grey by Floyd's father, Elwood Pyle. Grey's secretary was quite taken with the cubs, as were many who saw the friendly cubs, and enjoyed their antics. The author wrote several short stories inspired by the cubs. (Peace-Pyle collection.)

Lewie Pyle rewards the Pyle hound pack for putting a chicken-killing fox out of action. The lady displaying the fox was a friend of the noted author Zane Grey. (Peace-Pyle collection.)

Author Zane Grey (1872–1939) was a somber man at times, according to Richard Haught. Often during a hunt, his mind would stray to a story he was writing, and those around him learned not to distract him. Here he is pictured with his horse, Juan Carlos, at a hunting camp on top of the Mogollon Rim. (Peace-Pyle collection.)

Zane Grey brought his cook, George Takahashi, to the Rim Country on at least two occasions. It was told by Edd Haught and Floyd Pyle that Takahashi was a good camp cook and was a fair hand at cutting up meat brought in by the hunting parties. Takahashi disappeared after returning to California with Grey after one of his hunting trips, and his departure remains a mystery. (Courtesy NCGHS.)

Not all wild animals were captured for dinner or hides. "Pig Baby," the javelina, was a favorite pet of Myrtle Flack of Gisela. Although some people think javelina are a type of wild pig, they are actually part of the peccary family. (Peace-Pyle collection.)

Venison graced the tables of all the early settlers of the country Zane Grey called the Tonto Rim. Here Elwood Pyle has assured his family will eat well for the next week. When killed during the summer months, the meat was jerked (salted, peppered, and dried) to keep it from spoiling. (Peace-Pyle collection.)

Hunter Floyd Pyle trapped these 92 coyotes under the Mogollon Rim. Floyd was a paid government hunter and was asked to rid the country around Payson of bothersome coyotes. Note the ring-tailed cat at the extreme left of the photograph. Floyd had done his winter's duty with regard to the coyote population and was soon on the trail of a mountain lion or stock-killing bear, a much more befitting challenge. (Peace-Pyle collection.)

Here a child of the Rim Country watches as lion hunters prepare to depart the ranch in search of one of the big cats. He can hardly wait for the time when he will be old enough to ride on the hunt, an often-replayed event in the lives of the male children of the Rim Country. (Peace-Pyle collection.)

Jinx Pyle packed in this female lion on Jip, a two-year-old gelding. The lion was taken on top of Christopher Mountain and brought to the R Bar C Ranch. This was the first of over 50 mountain lions packed in on Jip by Jinx or his dad, Gene Pyle. (Peace-Pyle collection.)

For over a century, the men of the Pyle family were noted lion and bear hunters in the country around Payson. The big cats preyed upon deer and cattle, and ranching in the area would have been impossible had hunters not kept them under control. Here Malcolm Pyle is pictured on Yeller with a big tom caught in the Mazatzal Mountain Range southwest of Payson. (Peace-Pyle collection.)

Whenever Zane Grey came to his beloved Tonto Rim Country to hunt, he brought a party of his friends with him. This lady friend of the noted author is enjoying feeding the chickens at the Babe Haught Ranch after an early-fall snow. Coons, skunks, and foxes preyed on chickens, so they had to be shut up at night and watched during the daylight hours. No chickens meant no eggs for breakfast! (Peace-Pyle collection.)

David Gowan (left), founder of the Tonto Natural Bridge, and his grandniece, Anna Mae Ogilvie Deming, show the goose David caught for Thanksgiving dinner. This was 1921 on the Ogilvie Ranch in Star Valley. (Peace-Pyle collection.)

Gene (left) and Jinx Pyle trailed and ran this stock-killing bear for 9 miles before the hounds bayed him in the bluffs high under the Mogollon Rim above Bonita Creek. He had killed a baby calf and then killed the mother when she tried to fight him off the calf. (Peace-Pyle collection.)

Babe Haught was the official guide of Zane Grey in the Rim Country, but Haught's right-hand men were his son, Edd Haught (left), and Edd's best friend, Floyd Pyle. Floyd and Edd often hunted bear and lion together and are pictured here after a successful lion hunt. The lion across Floyd's saddle was taken near the Myrtle Ranch high up under the Mogollon Rim on Ellison Creek. (Peace-Pyle collection.)

Fishing was great on Tonto Creek south and east of Payson before 1958. Here Betty Russell, descended from the Pioneer Russell family of Payson and the surrounding country, has taken her limit. Each of these fish provided a meal for someone! Zane Grey also loved to fish. (Peace-Pyle collection.)

Plenty of mountain lions still make their home in the Rim Country near Payson. A few years ago, the prey base of the big cats consisted primarily of whitetail and mule deer with a few porcupines and other smaller animals to supplement their diet. Today elk are the primary food of the Rim Country mountain lion. The lion shown here is a big tom caught by Jimbo Armstrong with the aid of his hunting dogs. (Courtesy of Jimbo Armstrong.)

Bears often became cattle killers and were not tolerated on the ranches around Payson once they became known to possess the blood lust. These two were trailed from a calf they had killed by a Gisela Rancher, Ralph "Cuc" Hale, and paid the price for their transgression. (Peace-Pyle collection.)

These two hunters have stopped to have their pictures taken along the Control Road under the Mogollon Rim. They are on their way to the Myrtle Ranch where they will spend a week with Floyd Pyle on a guaranteed lion hunt. The fresh snowfall virtually guarantees the success of the hunt. (Peace-Pyle collection.)

A group of Payson cowboys prepares to join the Zane Grey hunting party at Turkey Springs. The rider at the far right is Lewis Pyle, and the other men are members of the Haught family. (Peace-Pyle collection.)

Here part of Zane Grey's Turkey Springs Camp is seen. Wild game in close proximity to the ranches under the Mogollon Rim was not as abundant as it was at some of the more remote areas. The Turkey Springs area was a favorite hunting location of Floyd Pyle who introduced it to the author. (Peace-Pyle collection.)

This elk was taken by the two men pictured who were guided by Edd Haught. They were with the Zane Grey party, and the only two of over 20 men in the party who cared to brave the snow that day. The meat was appreciated back at the Babe Haught Ranch. (Peace-Pyle collection.)

These local Payson cowboys, employed by Zane Grey, are packing supplies from a point near the Babe Haught Ranch on Tonto Creek to a hunting camp at Turkey Springs atop the Mogollon Rim. (Peace-Pyle collection.)

Zane Grey's camera crew is pictured under the Rim. Zane Grey first brought his movie company to the Mogollon Rim Country during the 1920s. Floyd Pyle, Lewis Pyle, and several members of the Haught family worked for Grey during the filming of *To the Last Man*, south of Payson, and also during the filming of *Wild Horse Mesa*, on top of the Mogollon Rim. Grey was not pleased with the quality of the films, as the existing technology was not up to the standards he required. He sold the company, which then became known as The Alaskans and later as Paramount Pictures. (Peace-Pyle collection.)

Four

RODEO

On the third weekend in August 1884, cowboys gathered and participated in the first Payson Rodeo. The event was held in the Mid-Town Pasture, southwest of the intersection of Old Main and Highway 87. The cowboys were anxious to see how their roping and riding skills compared to those of their neighbors. Horse racing, bronc riding, foot racing, and roping events, along with silver dollar pitching, dominated the early agenda. Through the years, steer busting, bulldogging, cowhide races, and other events were added. The Payson Rodeo soon became the premier social event of both the Rim Country and the lower Tonto Basin. It was a time when isolated ranch families could visit with their neighbors, many of whom they had not seen since the last rodeo.

The Payson Rodeo soon became as essential as Christmas to both the old-timers of the cattle industry and the folks in town. Payson's rodeo was socially and economically tied to the cattle industry. The continuity of the Payson Rodeo has survived world wars, depressions, recessions, and stock market crashes.

For the first 70 years of its existence, Payson was a wide-open, self-governing cow town. Due to the community's remote location, Payson folk had free rein to celebrate as they chose. The celebration went nonstop for four days with such activities as dancing, eating, fighting, and gambling taking over the festivities at night. The selling and drinking of White Mule thrived day and night during the four-day celebration.

Outside law was shunned, so Payson—especially during the August Celebration—was self-regulated and uninhibited. Through all the steer busting, cockfighting, betting, horse races, and fist fighting, Payson remained completely safe for women. Indeed, they were treated with great respect. The children participated in sack races, foot races, three-legged races, and even croquet. As soon as the festivities were over, many began counting the days until the next year's Payson Rodeo.

Charley Meadows was the primary founder and a favorite contestant in Payson's first rodeo held in August 1884. Just two years prior to his founding of the rodeo, his father, John M. Meadows, and brother, Henry Meadows, lost their lives in an Apache attack on the family's Diamond Valley Ranch, where the Whispering Pines subdivision is today. Arizona Charley Meadows billed himself as the world-champion cowboy for many years and made it stick by taking on and beating all comers at roping events. He was a star in various Wild West shows, including his own and Buffalo Bill's after he left the Payson area. (Peace-Pyle collection.)

Horse racing was a major part of the early Payson Rodeo. Some of the fastest horses in the world raced down Payson's Main Street or down the Lane, which was the road into town from the south. Thousands of dollars and even ranches, saddles, and cattle were won and lost at Payson rodeos back in the 1880s. Early horses of note were Desert, owned by the Houston brothers; Brown Dick; Crowder; and Butter and Honey. Later Payson-area racehorses included Buster, Prissy, Brown Bomber, Crusader, Clabber, and Tonto Gal. (Peace-Pyle collection.)

Many early rodeos took place right downtown on Payson's Main Street. People lined the streets making a human fence, which worked some of the time. At other times, a bovine critter would bust out followed by a cowboy. The animal might be roped in an adjacent meadow or on a hillside. No matter! It was all part of the show. (Peace-Pyle collection.)

Starting in the early 1920s, cars served double duty as fences and spectator seats. Here cars line Chilson's Field, where several early-day rodeos were held. It was easier on stock than the hard-packed granite of Main Street, but some years the field was too boggy for rodeo events due to summer rains. (Peace-Pyle collection.)

Earl Stephens was a noted Payson bronc rider during the 1920s and 1930s. He was a consistent winner in the rough-stock events and was also no man to tangle with in a fight. Here he shows his bronc-riding skills at Chilson's Field. (Peace-Pyle collection.)

Andy Ogilvie peaks through the fence at the old fairgrounds arena. Ola and Bill Wilbanks built the arena on their land just west of the main part of town in 1927, and the Payson Rodeo was held there until 1949. For many years, the Payson/Pine Fair was held under the grandstand during the rodeo. (Peace-Pyle collection.)

The grand entry signifies the beginning of a Payson Rodeo at the old fairgrounds arena. Fort McDonald Hill can be seen in the background. The hill was the site where Payson folks gathered in the early days to stave off Apache raids. The whole town and most of the country around can be seen from McDonald Hill. (Peace-Pyle collection.)

Cars line Main Street in Payson for a rodeo during the 1920s. The term "rodeo" did not come into consistent use until after 1930 in Payson. Before that, the Payson Rodeo was called the August Doins' or sometimes the World's Fair. Here we see tie-down calf roping as it was done in the 1920s. (Peace-Pyle collection.)

The cowhide race was a favorite Payson Rodeo event. Here Tom Morris rides the hide and Donnie Cline provides the horsepower. Unusual events such as the cowhide race, the wild cow milkin', and the wild horse race assured that almost anyone could participate in the rodeo and have a reasonable chance of winning. This event took place at the Y Arena northeast of downtown Payson. (Peace-Pyle collection.)

During the Y Arena's tenure, from 1950 through 1962, many of the best ropers in the world showed up in Payson to demonstrate their skills. Among them were Dale Smith, Oscar Walls, the Arnolds, Joe Bassett, the Schells, and more. Here we see Brad Smith in action. (Peace-Pyle collection.)

Gila County cowgirl Nancy Sheppard is the only woman ever to stand on the back of a running horse and spin two ropes at the same time. Here she does the trick while riding Roman style. Nancy is in the Cowboy Hall of Fame, the Cowgirl Hall of Fame, and the Pro Rodeo Hall of Fame for her riding and roping abilities. (Courtesy Nancy Sheppard.)

Payson's own Jim Kilby shows his skill and versatility by stepping in and out of a loop while spinning the cowboy wedding ring around his head. Jim preformed at many Payson rodeos and other events during the 1950s. (Peace-Pyle collection.)

Frank Kelly began riding bulls and broncs as a teenager and followed the rodeo circuit for almost half a century. Here he is shown on a bareback bronc at the Payson Rodeo in 1970. Also, he won the bull-riding event at a major rodeo in each of five decades. He was a contestant in the National Old Timer's Rodeo Finals in 1987 as part of the Senior Pro Tour, and he went to the Turquoise Circuit Finals in 1990. In 2009, he was inducted into the Payson Rodeo Legends Ring of Honor. (Courtesy Frank Kelly.)

Payson Rodeo boss Jim Barrett (left) and friend, Slim Anderson, put in many hours each year during the 1970s and 1980s to be sure that the World's Oldest Continuous Rodeo would never falter. Barrett got his start in 1959 volunteering on the Payson Jaycees Rodeo Committee to sell pop from the concession stands; then he served as rodeo boss from 1972 to 1884. Slim and Jim, both who have since passed on, represent many others who gave of themselves and their time to make the Payson Rodeo the best it could be. (Peace-Pyle collection.)

Eddie Conway of Payson and the lower Tonto Basin began riding bulls in 1959, when he graduated from high school, and made his living at the sport until 1965. Conway went to the National Finals Rodeo in both 1963 and 1964. He was a top-10 bull rider for 10 years. He also won the U.S. Team Roping Championship with his partner, John Ewing, in Oklahoma in 2001. In 2009, Conway was inducted into the Payson Rodeo Legends Ring of Honor as a charter member. (Courtesy Eddie Conway.)

Roy Honeycutt, longtime rodeo stock contractor, performer, and all-around cowboy is pictured here giving the opening prayer at the 1987 Payson Rodeo. For many years, both Payson and Prescott billed their rodeos as the world's oldest. To put an end to this, Prescott trademarked the phrase "World's Oldest Rodeo." With no other alternative, Payson trademarked "World's Oldest Continuous Rodeo" for its slogan. Payson Rodeo began in 1884, four years before Prescott's, and it continued uninterrupted throughout both World Wars. (Peace-Pyle collection.)

Local bull rider Doyle Crabtree is shown here on a rank one at the Payson Rodeo. Doyle is descended from the Crabtrees, one of the oldest and toughest pioneering families in Gila County and the Payson area. (Courtesy Doyle Crabtree.)

Rodeo is a very unpredictable sport, tracing its origin back to the everyday skills and crafts of the cowboy. Even the roping events can provide any number of wrecks, and with the "Rough Stock Events," some sort of mishap is virtually guaranteed. This roan horse is doing his best to keep up that tradition. (Peace-Pyle collection.)

Bronc riders and bull riders have a chance of landing on their feet, but with the sport of bulldogging, a man knows he is goin' to the dirt. This event requires great cooperation between the dogger, his horse, and the hazer. All must do their job, and do it well, for the effort to end in a successful run. Even then, sometimes a wise old steer will stop in his tracks at just the right instant and watch the riders and horses fly on by. (Peace-Pyle collection.)

The Mogollon Montoneras lent a helping hand at many rodeos. Here Connie O'Daniel (left) and Jeanne Henderson carry the flags into the arena to lead the grand entry. (Peace-Pyle collection.)

Jim Skinner is ready to rope a calf at the Payson Rodeo held at the Wilbank's Arena in August 1939. This was the first real rodeo arena built in Payson and the Payson-Pine was also held here under the grand stand. Prior to this arena, the rodeo was held on Main Street and in cattle pastures. Skinner was born in Payson and today, he and his wife, Joan, make their home in Payson not far from this arena. (Courtesy Jim Skinner.)

Five

MINING AND LOGGING

Although Payson was predominantly a cow town from its beginning in 1882 to about 1965, both the mining and the timber industries played a significant roll in its early economy.

Soon after the subjugation of the Apaches in the Tonto Basin, soldiers returned home and told of the rich native grasses and the promising mineral outcroppings in the area. The lure of gold and silver drew prospectors and miners into the basin. These men were usually single, and most of them came with a partner for companionship and to watch their back. Many of the early miners prospered, and it was supposed that the Oxbow Hill Country south of Payson as well as the country west of Payson into the Mazatzals would become a major mining mecca. But while the country yielded considerable wealth in the form of minerals, it fell short of the glowing predictions of the early miners. Gold can easily be retrieved from a rich lens of quartz running 6 inches wide on top of the ground. Twenty feet into the ground it becomes a different matter, as the muck on both sides of the rich ore must be moved, as well as the ore. Even so, several mines in the area including the Oxbow, Zulu, Golden Wonder, and the Grand Prize provided wage-earning jobs, and many knowledgeable mining men and prospectors were able to scratch out enough gold to live independently.

The timber industry also arrived early in Payson. Joseph S. Gibson felled trees on the Burch Ranch and split them into shakes that he sold in the Salt River Valley. Money from this endeavor gave him a start in the freighting and ranching business. The first sawmill was set up in Payson by its founders William Burch and William McDonald in 1880.

Many years later, Henry Haught set up a sawmill on the Control Road near the Diamond Point turnoff. This mill provided the lumber for many Rim Country barns and homes over the years and also milled the lumber for Zane Grey's cabin. In 1934, the Owens brothers began to mill lumber at their home then relocated the mill onto forestland in 1935. In 1951, the Owens mill was moved to Payson near the intersection of Main Street and Highway 87. The mill was sold to Kaibab Industries in 1958.

Several arrastras, first introduced to the New World by the Spanish in the 1500s, have been found in the Payson area. The word arrastra comes from the Spanish word *arrastre*, meaning to drag along the ground. When ore was quarried out of the hard-rock mines, the quartz had to be crushed to free the gold. The simplest form of the arrastra was a flat-bottomed drag stone placed in a circular, rock-lined pit and connected to a center post by a long arm. With a horse or mule providing power at the other end of the arm, the stone was dragged slowly around in a circle. Ore placed between the stone floor and drag stone was crushed into a coarse powder, after which water and quicksilver were added. The resulting slurry was then moved to troughs where the gold was recovered. (Courtesy NGCHS.)

Marysville, 1881, was located 3 miles west of Payson. Emer Chilson (right) started a store here to supply the miners and their families and named the place Marysville after his young daughter, Mary. About 100 people lived in Marysville in 1881, but due to an Apache scare, most of the people left. (Peace-Pyle collection.)

Tony and Lennie Menges and Bert Belluzzi (right) worked the Tonto Pittsburg Mine for many years. The Tonto Pittsburg Mine, which was a copper mine, was located south of Payson on Tonto Creek, where Hardt Creek runs into it. (Peace-Pyle collection.)

Wes Goswick was a lion hunter and a prospector. His lion hunting took him to the far reaches of the Tonto Basin and into country that even most prospectors might miss seeing. The big cats often climbed onto the cliffs and ledges of the mesas and high buttes to escape the hunting dogs, and it was in just such places that mineral-rich outcroppings were found. Goswick filed his first claim in 1886 and named it the Christmas Mine. He took considerable gold from this claim while he continued to prospect and support his family with his mining activities. Goswick moved to Roosevelt where he worked on the dam until the construction was finished. He later discovered and founded the Ord Mine with partners Bill Packard and Jess Henderson. He worked this mercury mine for several years until World War II, when it was no longer profitable. Goswick spent many of his remaining years living with his son-in-law, Alfred Packard, and his daughter, Belle. The two men hunted lion and continued prospecting until Goswick had a stroke in 1939. He passed away in May 1923. (Peace-Pyle collection.)

Wesley Goswick, Bill Packard, and Jess Henderson located what would become the Ord Mine on the north slope of Mount Ord in 1925. This rich mercury mine is about 20 miles south of Payson. The mine was developed in 1926 by the Arizona Quicksilver Corporation, who also constructed an ore-processing mill with a rotary furnace. The company built a wagon road up Slate Creek to the site, where it constructed a small town that was known as Goswick Camp. The mining boom was short lived, and Goswick Camp was abandoned after the Ord Mine and mill shut down in 1932. In the following years, the mine reopened several times, and a new mill was constructed closer to Slate Creek. (Peace-Pyle collection.)

This is one of the old Lousy Gulch Claims about 1.5 miles southeast of Payson. This picture is representative of many of the old mines in the Oxbow Hill Country. Ben Cole, with his sons, Emer and Pink, worked some mining claims in the gulch during the 1880s. Each night, the miners would have to get rid of the lice in order to sleep; therefore, both the claims and the drainage there became known as "Lousy Gulch." (Courtesy NGCHS.)

The Zulu Mine is located near the foot of Oxbow Hill, south of Payson. Bill Craig and Paul Vogel, who came to the Payson area in 1881, once owned this gold mine. While working the mine, they found one pocket of wire-gold ore and took out $7,000 worth of gold in a wheelbarrow. This gave them a start to found and stock the Spade Ranch, located on Webber Creek, north of Payson (now Camp Geronimo). (Peace-Pyle collection.)

This is a beautiful view of the rugged Mazatzal Mountains from the shaft at the 50-foot level of the Zulu Mine, located south of Payson on Oxbow Hill. The 40-mile-long Mazatzal Mountain Range is mineral rich and diggings from the early Spanish explorers can be found. Some were there long enough to build rock forts for protection from the marauding Apaches. The ore from the Zulu Mine was hauled to Globe to be milled until the 1940s. In the 1980s, modern equipment was brought in. The lighter-colored area in the picture above is where the topsoil was bladed to expose the gold ore. (Peace-Pyle collection.)

Walter Trezise (1910–1986) worked as a miner and a cowboy. He and his father lived in western New Mexico a few years then moved to Gisela, Arizona, in 1922. They lived in Gisela and worked on different ranches. In 1943, Trezise married Bennie Cooper, and they lived at his Oxbow mining claim for 20 years then moved back to Gisela. (Peace-Pyle collection.)

Walter Trezise bought his first mine in 1938 from H. J. Bratschi for $50. Located on Oxbow Hill, he called the mine the Garden. The mine was timbered with hand-hewn juniper posts. Trezise cut and hauled them in his pickup. He went down into the mine, put ore in a bucket, and then winched the ore out of the shaft with a windlass. Once the ore was extracted, Trezise hauled it to a mill near his house. A gasoline-powered mill pulverized the rocks, making it possible to extract gold, silver, and copper. Some might call this a primitive method of mining, but it supported Trezise all of his life. He also owned other mines: the Yellow Jacket, the Little Joe, and the Hornet, all in the same area. (Peace-Pyle collection.)

The discoverer of a lode had to record his claim in the recorder's office of the county where the lode was located within three months from the date of discovery. The lode claim certificate listed the name of the lode, name of the locator, name of location, the number of feet in length claimed on each side of the center shaft of the discovery, and the general course of the lode. (Courtesy NGCHS.)

Smoke bellows out of the burner of Owens Sawmill in Payson in the 1950s. The Bush Highway coming into Payson from Phoenix was not yet paved, so this photograph was taken before 1958. The only business along this section of the highway was Flack Brothers Garage that can be seen above and to the left of the burner. The sawmill was the main industry in Payson at this time. It provided jobs for many locals, and lots of timber under the Mogollon Rim made its way to the valley in the form of lumber. (Courtesy Ella Lee Owens.)

Keith Owens (left), along with his brother, Kerm, founded Owens Brothers Lumber in 1941. The brothers first had a portable mill under the Mogollon Rim. It was moved several times. In the late 1940s, after Keith had bought out his brother, the mill burned. Keith and his wife, Ella Lee, built a new mill in Payson but kept the Owens Brothers name. Keith was tragically electrocuted in January 1957, when a high-voltage line was struck with a crane on a log loader. He employed so many of the locals that the whole town mourned. Keith was highly respected. (Courtesy Ella Lee Owens.)

Ella Lee Owens, the wife of Keith, worked at his side. After his death, she took over the management of Owens Brothers Lumber and proved to be very competent. The mill was sold in December 1959 to Whiting and Kutch. (Courtesy Ella Lee Owens.)

Jim Deming, who later worked for Owens Brothers Sawmill, is notching a giant ponderosa pine so it will fall exactly where he chooses. Usually falling a tree of this size would be a job for two men with a crosscut saw, but for some reason, Jim is using an ax. The logging operation took place under the Mogollon Rim, and this great tree must have made a big stack of lumber at the old Haught Sawmill. (Courtesy Ella Lee Owens.)

Timber! Jim Kilby is felling a big ponderosa pine tree for Owens Brothers Lumber. Most of the homes in Payson were built from lumber milled by the Haught Sawmill or Owens Brothers Lumber until about 1970. (Courtesy Ella Lee Owens.)

Logging trucks like the one at left had to gear down to make it off the 1,000-foot drop to the foot of the Mogollon Rim. This load of logs is destined for the mill at Owens Brothers Lumber in Payson around 1955. (Courtesy Ella Lee Owens.)

Pete Haught and his sons, Henry, Charley, and Walter, bought a sawmill from Elam Boles in 1919 and moved it to Henry's homestead, now Tonto Village. The mill was sold to Mr. Standage in about 1942. (Peace-Pyle collection.)

Clayton Ashby is skidding logs to the loading site where they will await transportation to the mill in Payson. During the 1950s, Owens Brothers Lumber provided jobs for many Payson residents. The huge ponderosa pines made beautiful lumber when milled, and the Owens had both logging operations in progress and the mill running for many years. (Courtesy Ella Lee Owens.)

During most of the 1950s, Owens Brothers Lumber stood along the south side of Old Main Street, where Meadow Street intersects Old Main east to Highway 87. The mill occupied about 8 acres complete with a large mill pond, a large level area for drying stacks of lumber, and the great burner seen here at the top left of the photograph. (Courtesy Ella Lee Owens.)

Six

PAYSON AREA PERSONALITIES

The Tonto Basin of Arizona, which includes Payson, was the final stronghold of the Apaches in the United States. When it was opened for settlement after the General Crook campaign of 1872 and 1873, the first settlers were of a mixed breed. Some were outlaws looking for a new country where they would not be known or followed. Several were former Texas Rangers. More were Civil War veterans. There were bull whackers, muleskinners, miners, and cowboys. Some came to seek their fortunes and some to steal fortunes of others, but they had one thing in common: They were rugged individualists, for the Tonto Basin of 1874 was no place for the timid. Bronco Apaches continued their outbreaks and raiding through 1882 and beyond. Then at the close of the Apache raids came the Pleasant Valley War, a range war and feud between the Tewksburys and the Grahams in which some 40 men were killed.

Payson, the Rim Country, and the Tonto Basin also had many honest men and women who just wanted to be left to their honest pursuits of happiness. But these honest settlers had to be strong enough to cope with the outlaw faction, or they had to leave the country. The strength and diversity of Payson's early settlers assured that the ensuing generations would produce some characters, and so they did: men like George Cline, world-champion roper who tied the first calf in Madison Square Garden; Floyd Pyle, who took the first mountain lion alive for the San Diego Zoo; Arizona Charley Meadows, who preformed in Buffalo Bill's Wild West Show; and Tammy Kelly, six-time world-champion bull rider. Payson and the Tonto Basin were primarily cattle-ranching country through most of the 1960s and produced 10 world-champion cowboys.

As Arizona has grown so have Payson and the Tonto Basin. The Rim Country has experienced a major population expansion in the last 50 years, but plenty of salty characters can still be found in Payson and the surrounding area.

Hunter Haught (left), son of Shawn Haught, and Ned Barkley, son of Tommy Barkley, are seventh-generation members of their family to live in the Gisela Valley south of Payson. The boys are both descendents of Cornelius Jackson, who settled in Gisela in 1889, and Samuel A. Haught Sr., who settled under the Mogollon Rim in 1885. They are pictured here on the Gisela ranch where they lived as small children. (Peace-Pyle collection.)

Patricia "Pat" Neal Randall is a fourth-generation descendant of her family in the Payson area. She is the daughter of Buster and Ruby (Hilligass) Neal who owned the Doll Baby Ranch when she was young. Her children, grandchildren, and great-grandchildren also live in Arizona. Pat is married to Ronnie Randall and is active in her community. (Courtesy Pat Randall.)

In 1927, an MGM plane carrying Leo the Lion crashed in Hells Gate, south of Payson. Lewis Pyle helped move Leo the Lion from the point of the plane crash to the top of Mescal Ridge, where he could be transported by pickup into Payson. Dave Martin drove the pickup (above) to take Leo into Payson. The townspeople were in awe of an African lion, unlike the lions that were often caught in the Payson area. (Peace-Pyle collection.)

Lou Neal Pieper Jones arrived in Globe in 1889 with her two brothers, Will and Dan Neal, and her sister, Jane Neal Bohme. Lou had children to support so went to work starting her own ranch, from which she made a good living. Lou was a good cowboy and real handy with a rope. She roped at the rodeos in Gila County for many years, riding to Payson for the August Doin's as often as possible. Note the divided skirt she wore in public ropings. Lou was a lady . . . and a cowboy. (Peace-Pyle collection.)

Polly Brown is pictured here fanning up the branding fire with her hat. She was equally at home as a store owner, cowboy, barkeep, businesswoman, or rancher. She was burned out several times and had to start over, but Polly was no stranger to work. She did what had to be done. She participated in Payson's Main Street ropings and was honored as Payson's Rodeo Queen in 1966. (Peace-Pyle collection.)

Margaret "Babe" Haught Holder, daughter of Henry "Pappy" and Sarah "Mammy" Haught, grew up on a cattle ranch at Little Green Valley. She learned to rope with her brothers and was often a participant in Payson's Main Street rodeos. George Cline said that Babe Holder and Polly Brown were the "gen-u-wine" articles. If a calf could be roped, they would rope it. (Peace-Pyle collection.)

Belle Lovelady is best remembered by many folks as Payson's first Bell Telephone operator. Beginning in 1947, she spent 10 years on the job, and folks for miles around knew her voice on the old hand-crank lines. Belle recounts how those lines hummed and howled to the tune of the weather, but they were Payson's link with the outside world as well as with Pine, Young, and the faraway ranches under the Rim. (Peace-Pyle collection.)

When the owners of Payson's first golf course wanted to promote their new enterprise, they called on two of the town's celebrities to play a round of golf. Floyd Pyle, cowboy, rancher, renowned hunting guide, and all-around good sport, watches as Bill Boardman takes a whack at the ball. Calvin Peace and his D-4 Caterpillar built the golf course. (Peace-Pyle collection.)

Florence Packard settled at Greenback in the Tonto Basin with his father-in-law, David Harer, in 1874, when the Apaches were still on the loose. Packard and his wife, Sarah, had 11 children: Bill, Josie (Russell), Walter, Fred, Bertha (Schornick), Sophia (Darby), Alfred, Albert, Robert, Johnny, and Gus. Packard brought some of the first cattle into the Tonto Basin and started ranching with David Harer, who brought in hogs. When lion began killing their livestock, Packard brought in some dogs and spent a lot of time hunting. He killed more than 200 lions. When his kids were old enough to go to school, he moved down to Tonto Creek in the lower Tonto Basin and built a general store. He also kept bees and always had honey for sale in his store, along with horseshoes, flour, sugar, salt, coffee, etc. Sarah died in 1902. Packard died January 10, 1932, and is buried in the Cline Cemetery. Florence Packard was truly a pioneer of the first order. (Peace-Pyle collection.)

Local bull rider Harry Shill, pictured here around 1970, has several times parachuted out of an airplane into a rodeo arena before riding a bull. Harry has ridden bulls in rodeos for five decades and was inducted, as a charter member, into the Payson Rodeo Legends Ring of Honor in 2009. Shill is the Town of Payson's Official Rodeo Ambassador, so proclaimed by Mayor Kenny Evans in 2009 to promote the anniversary of the World's Oldest Continuous Rodeo. (Peace-Pyle collection.)

Shawn Haught, son of Butch Haught and Jayne Peace Pyle, has played in country dance bands in Payson and surrounding areas since he was 13 years old. The cow town of Payson was the social hub for a vast ranching community, and the Saturday night dances were the primary social activity of the town. Payson's early passion for music and dancing was handed down to younger generations and resulted in a demand for musicians. (Peace-Pyle collection.)

The Hale family has long been noted for its musicians. Ralph "Cuc" Hale could play a fiddle, guitar, mouth harp, accordion, or almost any other musical instrument handed to him. Cuc's son, Ralph Duke Hale, like his father, was musically talented and played for many country dances. Here, Taylor Hale, the son of Ralph Duke Hale, carries on the family tradition. Taylor is a member of the long-established Hashknife Band, and he plays with Clay Sopeland and Moonshine Mafia. Taylor is a good lead singer and one of the best bass guitar players in the business. (Peace-Pyle collection.)

Henry "Pappy" Haught was Zane Grey's inspiration for the fiddle-playing character in his great book *Code of the West*. For decades, the early Payson dancehalls rang as Pappy played the Rim Country's favorite home-grown ditty, "Rabbit, Where's your Mammy?" Here the late Billy "Whitebird" Haught, grandson of Pappy Haught, keeps the family fiddling tradition alive. (Peace-Pyle collection.)

For 50 years, beginning in the 1920s, the sweet refrain of Joe Hale's fiddle could be heard in the Gisela Valley or Down on the Blue on most any evening. Joe knew all the old songs that his family brought from Texas to Arizona, "Rubber Dolly," "The Blind Child," "Maiden's Prayer," and more, but he often made up his own tunes and words in the tradition of the old cowboys. (Peace-Pyle collection.)

John W. Wentworth was a noted early Payson attorney and politician. He once defended Al Rose and Miguel Apodaca in a Payson court for burning the Middleton Ranch House during the Pleasant Valley War. His fee was $600 and a $150 saddle horse. Wentworth became a judge and performed marriage ceremonies for many of the pioneering people in the Payson area. Wentworth married Katherine Houston, the sister of Sam, Andrew, and William Houston, who were early settlers in Star Valley. The couple had four children. Judge Wentworth died in Globe, Arizona, in 1954. (Peace-Pyle collection.)

John Henry Thompson came to the Rim Country, north of Payson, with Col. Jesse W. Ellison in 1885. After ranching for a few years at the head of Webber Creek under the Mogollon Rim, he acquired the handle of "Rim Rock" and, soon after, ran for sheriff of Gila County. His bid was successful, and he held the office of a county sheriff longer than anyone before or since. Here he is pictured (middle row in cowboy hat) with some of his deputies in Globe. (Peace-Pyle collection.)

Howard Childers (left) and Ronnie McDaniel both served years as Gila County deputies, and both also served as justice of the peace in Payson at the end of their stints as deputies. McDaniel was a deputy for about 20 years and a judge for about 20 years. Childers and McDaniel were two of the most liked and respected lawmen ever to serve Payson and the surrounding community. (Peace-Pyle collection.)

Seven

NATURAL BRIDGE

The world's largest natural travertine bridge is located 11 miles north of Payson, off Highway 87. The Tonto Natural Bridge, which provides a path across Pine Creek, is over 400 feet long, 180 feet high, and 150 feet wide at it widest point.

The first documentation of the bridge comes from Scotsman David Gowen in 1877. Gowen was heading up Pine Creek searching for a place to hide from Apaches, when he looked up and saw the bridge overhead. He built a small shack of logs and mud and planted an orchard, but he was a fiddle-footed wanderer and knew he would not settle at the bridge or anywhere else. He was, however, so impressed with the bridge that he wrote to his nephew, David Goodfellow, in Scotland to come build a home at the bridge. Goodfellow heeded his uncle's advice. He packed all the belongings he could carry, gathered his family, and sailed to New York. Then the Goodfellow family traveled across the United States to Flagstaff, Arizona, by steam-engine train. It was a weeklong trip from Flagstaff to the bridge in a freight wagon pulled by eight horses. In the wilds of Arizona, the Goodfellows built a house, barn, and guest lodge and planted a larger orchard. It took them three years to build a road down into the canyon, which greatly improved and added to the existing facilities. Lillias Goodfellow served meals to visitors for $1 each. The bridge became a popular resort with the local folks, and many weddings were held there. It changed hands a number of times over the years, and finally in 1990, it became the Tonto Natural Bridge State Park, owned and operated as a state park by the State of Arizona.

A waterfall drops 180 feet into Pine Creek from the top of the Tonto Natural Bridge. An orchard was planted on top of the bridge by David Gowen in the late 1870s. Apples, peaches, and apricots grew well here, and the bridge became noted for its delicious fruit. (Peace-Pyle collection.)

The area under the Tonto Natural Bridge is a rugged travertine gorge. Driftwood is often caught and wedged on the travertine ledges, left there by the flooding waters of Pine Creek. Visitors come from all over the world to visit this natural phenomenon. (Peace-Pyle collection.)

Ladders were constructed by early-day explorers beneath the Tonto Natural Bridge to make the hard-to-get-to places more accessible. Caves and blowouts abound beneath the bridge, and interesting formations grip the attention of those with curious minds. (Peace-Pyle collection.)

The rich soil on top of the Tonto Natural Bridge is ideal for a variety of fruit trees. The area is particularly conducive to the production of apples and apricots. It has, in fact, produced the largest apricot tree in the world; a fact which is noted in the *Guinness Book of World Records*. (Peace-Pyle collection.)

Women hiking at the natural bridge were not an unusual sight. Long dresses did not stop them from hiking up and down the trails to see the natural wonder. Big hats were the style of the day, and they protected their faces. (Peace-Pyle collection.)

Cascade Falls beneath the Tonto Natural Bridge is certainly a majestic sight. Spring water cascades in a steady stream down the banks, over moss-covered rocks and thick carpets of green fern, falling down to Pine Creek below. Behind the waterfall is a cave. (Peace-Pyle collection.)

Surrealistic travertine rock formations surround this visitor as he takes in the scenery beneath the Tonto Natural Bridge. Most who visit this marvel of Mother Nature are amazed at her artistic handy work. (Photograph by McCulloch, Peace-Pyle collection.)

The Lodge at the Tonto Natural Bridge provided early visitors with a lobby and dining room. Rooms could also be rented by those who wished to spend more time exploring the area or fishing for trout in Pine Creek. Note the deck on the roof of the lodge that provided a wonderful view of the canyon. (Peace-Pyle collection.)

The bridge also offered a campsite for those who wished to take advantage of the opportunity to enjoy the great outdoors. The rocky canyon walls rise from the tree-lined meadow, providing a sharp contrast in the landscape. Visitors never lacked for stunning views. (Peace-Pyle collection.)

David Goodfellow and his family made the Tonto Natural Bridge their home. Locally milled ponderosa pine trees provided the lumber for the Goodfellow home. Lillias Goodfellow, like many of her early-day neighbors, planted ivy, which grew to climb up the wall of this comfortable old porch. (Peace-Pyle collection.)

Lillias and David Goodfellow were hard-working pioneers, but they knew how to relax after a hard day's work. Here they rest at the front of cabins they built to rent out to the many visitors to the bridge. (Peace-Pyle collection.)

Many of Payson's best have been married at the Tonto Natural Bridge. Here Anna Mae Ogilvie and Jim Deming continue the tradition. Anna Mae's sister, Beryl Ogilvie, was maid of honor, and Dave Goodfellow served as best man. The Demings were married on July 15, 1933. (Peace-Pyle collection.)

The Tonto Natural Bridge was quite remote, and supplies had to be hauled in to accommodate the considerable tourist trade of the lodge. The Goodfellows often made trips to Flagstaff to purchase supplies. Here they are at the top of the Mogollon Rim on their return trip to the lodge. (Peace-Pyle collection.)

Pausing for a photograph under the Tonto Natural Bridge are, from left to right, (first row) unidentified and Myrl Pyle; (second row) two unidentified, Myrth Pyle, Laura Beard, and Jesse Chilson. The Pyle twins were the inspiration for Zane Grey's book *Twin Sombreros*, and both danced with the noted author at numerous Rim Country dances. (Peace-Pyle collection.)

Shown here, Pine Creek winds its way along under the Tonto Natural Bridge. The vegetation is diverse along the creeks of the Rim Country, and even in the shaded area of the bridge, it is dense and beautiful. The boulders and rocks afford a rugged majesty to the scene. (Courtesy Jim Skinner.)

A different view of the bridge can be seen from the east wall of the canyon as one looks north up the creek. This must be close to the view David Gowen had with his first encounter of the bridge. (Courtesy Jim Skinner.)

Harry and Beryl Goodfellow were married at the Tonto Natural Bridge in 1911. As with all the early weddings at the bridge, elegance and the natural beauty of the wild canyon combine to make a beautiful picture. (Peace-Pyle collection.)

George Francis "Frank" Herron (front right), his wife, Mary Ellen "Molly" Herron (front left), and family are shown picnicking at the Tonto Natural Bridge during a family outing around 1900. Their daughter, May Herron (back row right), was a local schoolteacher who married John Lazear of Pine. The Herrons' son, Francis, is seated on the left in the back row. The Herrons ran cattle on the Moqui Ranch. (Peace-Pyle collection.)

David and Lillias Goodfellow are pictured atop the Mogollon Rim. David is pointing to their home at the Tonto Natural Bridge. (Peace-Pyle collection.)

This old piano was freighted into the Tonto Natural Bridge by team and wagon. Many guests have been entertained, and many couples have danced to the chime of its ivory keys. (Courtesy NGCHS.)

Eight
Transportation

Wagon roads were few and the surrounding mountains were tall, rough, and steep, so the primary means of transportation in the Payson area before 1900 was by horseback. Flour, salt, and other necessities were brought in by pack-train. Freight wagons rolled into Payson during the early years. Those freight wagons arriving from the Salt River Valley to the south of Payson had to travel up Fish Creek Hill and navigate the Apache Trail, another very formidable route. The burro trains of Elwood and Lewis Pyle could make the trips in half the time and were more reliable, as the burros had no wheels or axles to break.

As roads were improved and shortened, freight wagons replaced the burro trains and more buggies and buckboards were seen entering Payson. Ore was sometimes hauled from the local mines to the mills in Globe by freight wagons. By 1925, several Payson families had cars, although buggies, wagons, and horses were still the primary source of transportation. Wagons were still used to haul logs to the mills, and burros packed lumber over the trail to the old Babe Haught Ranch to be used in the building of Zane Grey's cabin.

During the 1930s, gas-driven trucks gradually replaced the freight wagons. In Payson, cars became more prevalent than buggies or buckboards. The transition to motorized vehicles took place slower in Payson than other parts of the country, again due to the isolation and rough country.

Payson caught up with the rest of the world after World War II. Ranchers, miners, and town folk had cars and pickups. Logs, lumber, and cattle were hauled in trucks. By the 1930s, an occasional plane landed in the Rim Country. By the 1950s, Payson had an airport runway, and during the 1960s, there were three separate local landing strips.

During the 1950s, it was still an eight-hour drive from Phoenix to Payson over the old Bush Highway, but gradually the road was improved; the curves were taken out, and the new Beeline Highway was paved in 1958. That same year, Main Street was paved in Payson, and from that point on, transportation was little different than in most modern towns and cities.

May Herron Lazear was a schoolteacher and a great lady of the Rim Country and Payson. She also had an interest in the old Herron Hotel in Payson and worked there when she was not teaching. Lazear, like many of the early Payson women, was equally at home on the back of a horse or on foot. (Peace-Pyle collection.)

Doubtful Canyon is 20 miles east of Payson between the R Bar C Ranch and Kohl's Ranch. It earned the name because anytime there was very much rain or snow, it was doubtful if it could be crossed with a team and wagon, and the same doubts remained for many years after vehicles were in use. (Courtesy NGCHS.)

Freight wagons brought supplies into Payson from both Flagstaff and the Salt River Valley starting in about 1890, but pack animals were common carriers of goods until about 1900. Roads into Payson from the north or south crossed rough country, and pack animals could make the journeys much faster than wagons because they did not have to follow the winding roads. (Courtesy NGCHS.)

This early-day vehicle appears to be taking the place of a couple of good packhorses. Its owner has been in the General Merchandise store buying supplies and will soon be on the road home. (Courtesy NGCHS.)

Ruby Hilligass Neal is shown riding a large workhorse with considerable Belgian blood. Payson pioneers got the most use possible from their horses. This versatile animal could carry a lady to town and back then be hooked to a plow or cultivator to do a little farm work or even pull a buggy. (Courtesy Pat Randall.)

The kids filled the car and there was no trunk, so some innovative soul built a sideboard from the front to the back fender. Using the running board for a bottom, he made a place to carry some much-needed cargo. (Peace-Pyle collection.)

These gents are reliving one of the earlier modes of transportation in the Rim Country and Payson. (Peace-Pyle collection.)

This gasoline wagon has undergone a considerable amount of renovation. Walter Trezise (left) was a miner and an innovative mechanic. He needed tall wheels for clearance to get into his backcountry mining operations. It also appears he may have been the original inventor of bucket seats. His companion on this excursion is Payson storekeeper Bill Boardman. (Courtesy NGCHS.)

Rim Country people were very isolated and innovative. They had to make do with what they had. With the tractor broken down, they put the tractor wheels on the family car so they could plow. (Courtesy NGCHS.)

Andy Ogilvie is disking up a field at his farm in Star Valley, east of Payson. Four of the main crops planted in the Payson area under this type of cultivation were corn, winter wheat, Blue Ribbon sorghum cane, or milo maze. (Peace-Pyle collection.)

The Ogilvie family is loaded up and headed for Payson in the family car. (Peace-Pyle collection.)

The old Model A and Model T cars with the gravity-fed gas systems had to be backed up some of the steep grades encountered on Oxbow Hill between Payson and Roosevelt. This man's wife has learned to drive the family car. (Peace-Pyle collection.)

Florence Packard is parked at the front of the store he built in the lower Tonto Basin at Punkin Center. Florence was a rancher and a lion hunter but moved into the lower basin and became a storekeeper so his children could attend school. (Peace-Pyle collection.)

Author-historian Jayne Peace Pyle was raised on a cattle ranch 17 miles south of Payson at Gisela, an early Mormon settlement. Here she rides with her family looking for wild cattle in the Four Peaks of Arizona in 1991. Jayne is married to author-historian Jinx Pyle. (Peace-Pyle collection)

Richard Taylor, son of Dick Taylor of the Doll Baby Ranch, shown horseback on the lower East Verde River east of Payson, is ready to roundup the pasture and corral the cattle in 1915. Ranch kids were expected to help with the family cattle operations at an early age. (Courtesy NGCHS.)

These women from a ranch south of Payson wait for their husbands so they can drive into Payson for a weekend of dancing, visiting, and fun. (Courtesy NGCHS.)

This gentlemen and his friend take a break from ranch work to try out the new one-horse buggy he bought for the missus. (Courtesy NGCHS.)

Setting charges of dynamite so a road could be constructed through the Mazatzal Mountains was a tough job. The Bush Highway, which connected Payson to Phoenix, was built in the 1930s. Before this stretch of road was completed, people had to drive over the treacherous Reno Road or through Roosevelt and over the Apache Trail to get from Payson to Phoenix. (Peace-Pyle collection.)

Most Payson children had their own modes of transportation. If a horse was not available, a wagon or a sled usually was. All they needed was a pull or a push. (Peace-Pyle collection.)

Pilot Martin Jensen was flying MGM's Leo the Lion from Los Angeles to New York in 1927, when his plane crashed in Hell's Gate, southeast of Payson. The African lion was in a cage that was welded to the plane. The cage protected the lion, and he was hauled out of Hell's Gate Canyon and taken into Payson. While he waited for a ride back to Los Angeles, the Payson townspeople went to see the lion. (Peace-Pyle collection.)

In 1935, the first airplane landed in Payson. It was piloted by Cliff Edwards (left), pictured above with his co-pilot, Floyd Hanson. Edwards authored a book of his experiences called *Horseback and Airborne*. (Courtesy NGCHS.)

Nine
WATER

Water has long held a fascination for all those who live in the arid state of Arizona, even those who live in the mountain towns like Payson. The cool running trout streams of the mountains are a delight to all who see them. The mountain lakes are peaceful and pleasant to the eye, and the springs are vital to wildlife, as well as to people and livestock. The early settlers followed the streams and built their homes nearby. They diverted the water into ditches and canals to provide irrigation. They built the dams on the mountain streams to control the flooding and to provide water for the desert cities. Lake-related recreation is also a vital part of Arizona's culture, and statistics show that Arizona has more boats per capita than any state in the union. It is a case of supply and demand; the less we have of something, the more we come to appreciate it.

Arizona is also a land of violent thunderstorms, summer rains, and flash floods. Cool mountain streams and even dry arroyos and canyons can be filled with raging torrents of water in seconds. Many have drowned in Tonto Creek, Christopher Creek, and in the sometimes-angry waters of the East Verde River. Some have simply been caught unaware by flash floods. Others have foolishly tried to cross these and other waters in flood stage and have been dragged down and rolled along the canyon bottoms with the river boulders. The waterways in the Payson area are sometimes peaceful and tranquil; other times they can be wild and raging. In either case, water in the Rim Country and the Tonto Basin, as well as in all of Arizona, is like a beautiful woman. It is to be loved and respected.

The East Verde River was referred to as the "East Fork of the Verde" in King Woolsey's Report of June 2, 1864, but the early maps refer to it as the East Fork of the Rio Verde. Starting under the Mogollon Rim, it flows southwest, picking up many tributaries before it empties into the main Verde River at the north end of the Mazatzal Range. (Photograph by McCulloch, courtesy Peace-Pyle collection.)

The waters of Christopher Creek churn in flood stage through a box canyon on their journey to merge with Tonto Creek. Christopher Creek was named after Isadore Christopher, founder of the C. I. Ranch under the Mogollon Rim and on the banks of the creek that bears his name. Today Christopher Creek is also the name of a small community that plays host to many tourists and vacationers. (Peace-Pyle collection.)

Early settlers made use of whatever form of power was available. Here a flume carries water from the East Verde River to a water wheel. The wheel powers the generator from an old car. The generator charges batteries, which in turn provide power for DC light bulbs that light the house. (Peace-Pyle collection.)

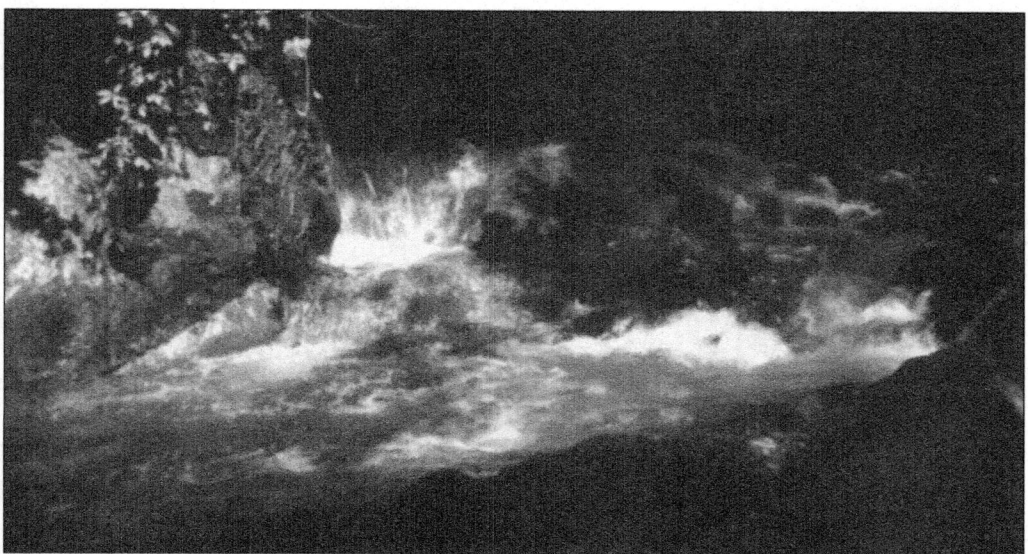
The waters of this warm spring at Fossil Creek are highly mineralized. Although Fossil Creek Canyon is deep and the area of the warm springs is not easily accessible, it is frequented by many who wish to enjoy a soak in its warm waters. The springs are only about 30 miles northwest of Payson, but the winding road into the canyon makes it almost double that distance. (Peace-Pyle collection.)

Here the waters of Tonto Creek, at the lower end of the box canyon below the Gisela Valley near Payson, run muddy after the summer rains. Note the Saguaro cactus on the point jutting into the bend of the creek. (Photograph by Walt Dice, courtesy Peace-Pyle collection.)

Roosevelt Lake now covers the old pioneer town of Livingston that was located where Tonto Creek joined the Salt River. Moonlight shimmers on the water and the Sierra Anchas provide a beautiful backdrop. (Photograph by McCulloch, courtesy Peace-Pyle collection.)

Lake Mary, on the road from Payson to Flagstaff, is a significant landmark along the way. Many a camp was made here by Payson pioneers on their way to and from Flagstaff to buy supplies. (Photograph by Ralph Fisher, courtesy Peace-Pyle collection.)

Melting snows cause Ellison Creek to rise, sending its rushing waters toward Pyeatt Draw, to Cold Springs, and on to the East Verde River. Other creeks that head under the Mogollon Rim and drain into the East Verde include Lewis Creek, Chase Creek, Webber Creek, Bonita Creek, Perley Creek, and Pine Creek. (Peace-Pyle collection.)

Tonto Creek is shown here in flood stage as it rushes through Gisela on its way to Roosevelt Lake. In Payson, the Rim Country, and the Tonto Basin a slow meandering stream or even a dry wash can become a raging torrent in a matter of minutes, sometimes seconds. (Photograph by Walt Dice, courtesy Peace-Pyle collection.)

Andy Ogilvie (right) and Harry Goodfellow cook the trout they caught in Bonita Creek under the Mogollon Rim. Bonita Creek, often called Pyle Creek by Zane Grey and others, was named Bonita by Elwood Pyle. He named his ranch Bonita Gardens. (Peace-Pyle collection.)

The wonderful little trout stream of Bonita Creek has provided a pleasant day of fishing for many Payson folks. Often a picnic followed a morning of fishing, as it did here with Theresa Boardman (seated by the tree) and her friends. (Peace-Pyle collection.)

Ellison Creek on the Myrtle Ranch sings along through a grove of poplar trees on a winter day under the Mogollon Rim. Those who live in the area very much appreciate the live streams that grace the surrounding mountain country and beautify the land. (Peace-Pyle collection.)

Through the 1950s, fishing was extremely good throughout Payson area. This couple appears to have caught more fish than they could eat, something easy to do in the early days of the Rim Country. (Peace-Pyle collection.)

Bridges like this one across Rye Creek now serve as only a scenic diversion to the natural landscape. In years past, the Rye Creek Bridge saved many miles of driving in good weather and made crossing the creek possible during the frequent times of high water. (Peace-Pyle collection.)

In its upper reaches under the Mogollon Rim, Tonto Creek is a trout stream. Carp and bass become more dominant as it flows into the Gisela Valley, winding its way out of the mountains and into lower country before entering Roosevelt Lake. (Courtesy NGCHS.)

The Childers family crossed Tonto Creek in the lower Tonto Basin on the old road from Globe to Payson. Ernest Piper rides horseback at the front of the wagon to be sure the chosen route holds no dangerous surprises for those in the wagon. (Courtesy NGCHS.)

Area streams were often formidable obstacles for travelers before the bridges were built. Here the Goodfellow family enlists the help of a team of horses to pull their car across a muddy creek. (Peace-Pyle collection.)

Cattle on their way to market, or during roundups, regularly had to swim creeks and rivers. Tonto Creek, the East Verde River, and Salt River often ran wide and deep, but the cattle could easily cross by swimming. (Peace-Pyle collection.)

Houston Creek, named after the Houston brothers of Star Valley, starts above Star Valley, runs through it, and empties into Tonto Creek at the north end of Gisela. In this photograph, Bishop Knoll, or Bishop's Nose, as the early Mormon settlers called it, can be seen. (Courtesy NGCHS.)

The old Theodore Roosevelt Dam is built of native rock and holds back the waters of Roosevelt Lake at full capacity. The old road went over the dam and was too narrow for cars to pass. Note the old canal on the left. (Courtesy NGCHS.)

Dogs, like kids, enjoy running and sliding on the frozen ponds in the Payson area. This pond is on the old Wade Ranch. These ponds provide fishing and swimming in the warmer-weather months. (Courtesy Jim Skinner.)

Ten
PAYSON BUILDINGS

Payson's earliest buildings were constructed of logs and chinked with mud. Before Payson was a town, however, William Burch and William McDonald had invested in a sawmill, so many older buildings in the area were often constructed in board-and-batten style. Board and batten is a type of exterior siding that has alternating wide boards and narrow wooden strips, called battens. The battens are nailed over the seams between the wider boards. Most were not fancy but were built to the no-nonsense standards of the day. Because they were heated with open fires and lit with candles or kerosene lamps, most did not survive and, at some point, burned to the ground. Others were invaded by termites and some, built on the ground, simply rotted.

In 1904, the first commercial rock building, Boardman's Mercantile, was completed. It was built from Payson's native red sandstone, which was quarried from a rock pit that is now on the Tonto Apache Reservation. Boardman's Mercantile also housed the U.S. Post Office.

Still several sawmills existed through the years in or near Payson and the great ponderosa pines were plentiful, so most of Payson's buildings continued to be constructed of lumber. Many burned including the 16 to 1 Saloon, Herron Hotel, Pioneer Bar, and the Elk Bar and Dancehall, which had years later been renamed the Winchester. The Old Barkdoll Dancehall burned, was rebuilt, and burned again. Many of the older homes simply outlived their usefulness and were torn down to make way for new construction.

In 1937, the WPA built what is now the Julia Randall School out of the same native red sandstone as was earlier used to build Boardman's Mercantile. This building still stands today, although is surrounded by new construction and not easily visible.

Because most all of Payson's early buildings were constructed from wood, and wood structures tend not to last like brick and stone, very few Payson buildings have survived over 100 years. But the old photographs still give us a picture of how Payson looked in days gone by.

During the 1890s, the new Herron Hotel (left) was a popular place in Payson. People could rent a room in the two-story building and eat at the Stewart Restaurant located just to the west of it. Frank and Molly Herron built the Hotel and their daughter, May, worked there cleaning rooms, waiting tables, and cooking food. May later married John Lazear of Pine. Wagons and buggies brought people from the outlying areas into Payson to get mail, visit, and buy supplies. (Peace-Pyle collection.)

August Pieper Saloon (right) is now Bootleg Alley Antiques on Main Street in Payson. Babe Haught is standing between the wagon tracks. The men are gathered here awaiting a horse race. (Peace-Pyle collection.)

J. W. Boardman Mercantile and the Hilligass Boarding House are shown prior to 1915. The boarding house is now the Lone Pine Hotel. (Peace-Pyle collection.)

Boardman's Mercantile, a gas station, and the Lily Ice Cream Shop on Payson's Main Street are shown around 1930. Boardman Brothers leased out their rock building on the corner of Main Street and Old Pine Road and built a store next to the gas station on Main Street. Dorothy Pyle, born in 1920, can recall being in the ice cream shop when she was five years old. (Peace-Pyle collection.)

Castle and Hubert, previously the Boardman Brothers rock store, had a handy gas pump in 1932. The gas was hauled in from Globe. Looking east on Main Street, one can see the huge cottonwood tree in front of the Pioneer Bar. (Peace-Pyle collection.)

The Payson Lodge is a prime example of early Payson architecture. It was constructed from huge pine logs, and the porch roof was made from split pine logs. This was later the site of the Pioneer Bar, another historic wood building that burned. (Peace-Pyle collection.)

From left to right are the gas station, Levi Cooper's Barbershop, Levi Cooper's house, and Boardman's Store. Levi Cooper lived in this little house on Payson's Main Street and raised a son, Levi Cooper Weigand, there. His barbershop was next door. The barbershop and Cooper's house burned between 1930 and 1935. Cooper then lived at Turkey Springs. He started another barbershop in the Old Elks. (Peace-Pyle collection.)

Boardman Brothers General Merchandise was located on Payson's Main Street. J. W. Boardman had a general store in Rye starting in the 1880s. His wife, Mary, was the postmistress. Mary returned to San Diego in 1885 to have her oldest son, Bill, and she returned again in 1886 to have her younger son, Guy. These were long trips by wagon, but Mary wanted to have proper medical facilities. In the 1890s, Boardman built a new store in Payson. His boys grew up learning the store business. When he retired, Bill and Guy Boardman built a new store and post office on Payson's Main Street (above). It also housed the post office, and Bill served as postmaster for 25 years. (Peace-Pyle collection.)

Bill Boardman was an upstanding citizen in Payson. He learned the mercantile business from his father at an early age, and then he and his brother, Guy, operated their own stores along Payson's Main Street. In 1912, Bill married Theresa Haley, a nurse who helped Dr. Christian Risser care for the people in the Payson area. (Peace-Pyle collection.)

The Roundup Malt Shop on Main Street was the place for young people to gather. It was the only place in Payson that had ice cream. (Peace-Pyle collection.)

Mary Lynn Skinner, her main means of transportation, and her collie dog are pictured in front of the old Pioneer Bar on Payson's Main Street in the 1930s. The Pioneer was the site of many Saturday night dances in Payson, and it was packed during the August rodeos. Pappy Haught, Joe Hale, Bill Haley, Rose Childers, Clyde Sellers, and other locals played for the dances. (Courtesy Jim Skinner.)

The Payson ranger house and station were here in 1907. The house (left) was rebuilt in 1933. Today the house is the gift shop of the Northern Gila County Historical Society. The back of the ranger station now houses the library and archives. The front looks much as it did when the ranger worked there. The U.S. Forest Service moved their office in 1974 and deeded the land to the Northern Gila County Historical Society in 1985. A replica of the Herron Hotel was built between the house and ranger station in 1985 and houses the Northern Gila County Historical Society Museum. (Courtesy NGCHS.)

Fred Croxen was Mazatzal District and Payson District ranger from 1910 through 1930. While in the Payson area, he interviewed many old-timers and documented their histories and biographies. His *Grazing on the Tonto National Forest*, written in 1926, has been a great source of information. (Courtesy NGCHS.)

Teachers Julia Randall (left) and Leona Fuel are pictured with their class on the steps of the Rock School Building in 1949. This school was later named the Julia Randall Elementary School in honor of Julia Randall, who taught three generations of students in the Payson area over 50 years. (Peace-Pyle collection.)

Payson High School (left) and Payson Grade School were located just east of where the Presbyterian Church is today. Land for the schools was donated by James Marshall Azbill and Jesse Chilson. Note the well and the flagpole in the front. (Peace-Pyle collection.)

This cabin was built for the filming of the *Life and Times of Grizzley Adams* in Payson during the 1970s. The filming of the television and film series, starring Dan Haggerty and Denver Pyle, caused quite a commotion in Payson. Many Paysonites were hired as extras; Jan Chilton and her two kids, Denise and Butch, were among them. The series was loosely based on a true story. Grizzly Adams (Haggerty) was a woodsman during the frontier era who fled into the mountains after he was wrongly accused of murder. While struggling to survive, Adams discovered an orphaned grizzly bear cub that he took in and named Ben. The bear, despite its huge adult size, became Adams's closest companion. (Peace-Pyle collection.)

Julia Randall and Theresa Boardman lay the cornerstone of the new Payson Woman's Club building in 1948. The Payson Woman's Club is the oldest service club in Northern Gila County. Payson Woman's Club was founded in 1921, when a group of Payson women went to work having bake sales to raise money so the town could have a sundial. (Peace-Pyle collection.)

With first-president Lena Chilson at the helm, the Payson Woman's Club began contributing to the community in many ways. Each Christmas, the women made gifts for everyone. The club acquired ownership of the Payson Pioneer Cemetery and had a bridge built across American Gulch. They established a library for the town and acquired a gold mine. Today Payson Woman's Club still works hard to help the community. (Peace-Pyle collection.)

The Payson schoolhouse, shown in 1904, was built of milled lumber from one of the local sawmills and constructed in the board and batten style. Note the glass windows. (Courtesy Peace-Pyle collection.)

Steve and Cindy Hathaway's Trading Post was located on Payson's Main Street in the 1940s. (Courtesy Pat Randall.)

Connolly's Store, ran by Harry and Merrelle Connolly in the 1940s, was located on the south side of Main Street and was connected to Hathaway's Trading Post. (Courtesy Pat Randall.)

The Elk Bar, located on the south side of Main Street, was once owned by Howard Childers (in white shirt), who also owned the NB Ranch on the lower East Verde River. This was during Payson's heyday as a cow town. Howard was a strong supporter of the Payson Rodeo, and the money made from the slot machines in the bar went to support the rodeo. (Peace-Pyle collection.)

The Oxbow Saloon on Payson's Main Street (right) is seen as it appeared in the late 1960s. The early Payson rodeos were held in cow pastures and on Main Street. Since the Payson Rodeo began in 1884, the dances were held on Main Street, and the thousands who have attended can probably recall a few fights to go along with the fun. (Peace-Pyle collection.)

The Oxbow Saloon is still open today and is on the National Register of Historic Buildings. It was built by Willie Wade and Dolph McKamey in 1932. (Peace-Pyle collection.)

Visit us at
arcadiapublishing.com

CPSIA information can be obtained
at www.ICGtesting.com
Printed in the USA
LVOW04*2102051217
558778LV00021B/75/P